T0194155

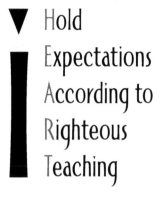

Hold Expectations According to Righteous Teaching

30-Day Devotional

TIFFANY WHITE

WESTBOW
PRESS®
A DIVISION OF THOMAS NELSON
& ZONDERVAN

WestBow Press books may be ordered through booksellers or by contacting:

WestBow Press
A Division of Thomas Nelson & Zondervan
1663 Liberty Drive
Bloomington, IN 47403
www.westbowpress.com
1 (866) 928-1240

Because of the dynamic nature of the Internet, any web addresses or links contained in
this book may have changed since publication and may no longer be valid. The views
expressed in this work are solely those of the author and do not necessarily reflect the
views of the publisher, and the publisher hereby disclaims any responsibility for them.

Any people depicted in stock imagery provided by Thinkstock are models,
and such images are being used for illustrative purposes only.
Certain stock imagery © Thinkstock.

Scripture quotations are taken from the Holy Bible, New Living Translation, copyright
©1996, 2004, 2007, 2013, 2015 by Tyndale House Foundation. Used by permission of
Tyndale House Publishers, Inc., Carol Stream, Illinois 60188. All rights reserved.

Scripture quotations marked (NIV) are taken from the Holy Bible, New International Version®,
NIV®. Copyright © 1973, 1978, 1984, 2011 by Biblica, Inc.™ Used by permission of Zondervan.
All rights reserved worldwide. www.zondervan.com The "NIV" and "New International Version"
are trademarks registered in the United States Patent and Trademark Office by Biblica, Inc.™

Scripture quotations marked (AMP) are taken from the Amplified Bible, Copyright ©
1954, 1958, 1962, 1964, 1965, 1987 by The Lockman Foundation. Used by permission.

Scripture quotations marked (NIrV) are taken from the Holy Bible, New International
Reader's Version®, NIrV® Copyright © 1995, 1996, 1998, 2014 by Biblica, Inc.™
Used by permission of Zondervan. All rights reserved worldwide. www.zondervan.
com The "NIrV" and "New International Reader's Version" are trademarks
registered in the United States Patent and Trademark Office by Biblica, Inc.™

Scripture taken from the New King James Version®. Copyright © 1982
by Thomas Nelson. Used by permission. All rights reserved.

Scripture quotations marked MSG are taken from THE MESSAGE, copyright ©
1993, 1994, 1995, 1996, 2000, 2001, 2002 by Eugene H. Peterson. Used by permission
of NavPress. All rights reserved. Represented by Tyndale House Publishers, Inc.

ISBN: 978-1-5127-8769-6 (sc)
ISBN: 978-1-5127-8768-9 (hc)
ISBN: 978-1-5127-8770-2 (e)
Library of Congress Control Number: 2017907615

Print information available on the last page.

WestBow Press rev. date: 5/10/2017

Contents

Preface

Wherever your treasure is, there the desires of your heart will also be. (Matthew 6:21 NLT)

Introduction

My primary reason for writing this devotional is to let *you* know that no matter what people have said about you, what the world has labeled you as, or what you've told yourself, anything is possible when you refocus your mind and align it with the expectations of our Father. So, do me a favor: Get rid of all the clutter and trash that cloud your mind and prepare yourself to be filled with God's Knowledge.

iHeart]

iHeart is a ministry that was birth in my heart six years ago. In 2012, God gave me the name and the mentorship program was launched shortly after. iHeart stands for iHold Expectations According to Righteous Teaching. God gave me wisdom where I was able to relate to the need in my community on many different levels. *Finally,* I realized why I had to go through so much emotionally and physically; it was God's way of birthing a ministry through me.

Jeremiah 29:11 says:

For I know the plans I have for you," declares the Lord, "plans to prosper you and not to harm you, plans to give you hope and a future. (NIV)

Our difficulties and challenges in life prepare us for the future that God has already planned. Your past, and your current state is nothing to hide or anything to be ashamed of. Rather, it's something to confront. I spent many nights (and days) crying because I didn't understand why I was so different and why I felt *so* out of place. I couldn't figure out why everyone else loved me; because truth of the matter was I hated myself; and many of you are in the same position. I magnified every negative thing about myself. So, my vision was clouded from who I truly was. It was clouded from who

God originally made me to be. I felt out of place because I couldn't see who I was, therefore I didn't know where I belonged. *Selah*

But I want to encourage you to realize the beauty within you. You are beautiful in God's eyes. So, clear the clutter clouding your mind and prepare to go on a journey that will bring clarity, healing, and confidence.

1

Lifestyle

Day 1: Salvation

> If you declare with your mouth, "Jesus is Lord,"
> and believe in your heart that God raised him from
> the dead, you will be saved. For it is with your heart
> that you believe and are justified, and it is with
> your mouth that you profess your faith and are
> saved. (Romans 10:9–10 NIV)

Here we are: Day 1. Let's start with the basics. Let's start by asking a question that many are afraid to ask. Are you confident that you will spend eternity in hell? I know—not what you expected! But think of it this way: Many people know that heaven exists, but they bypass the fact that hell is just as real as heaven. Who wants to go there? If you have not given thought about reclaiming your authority as a daughter to our Father, then you have signed yourself up to burn in hell. Yes, hell is *real*!

Application
Ask yourself this:

Do I know Jesus as my Savior?
Will I live in heaven?
Will God say well done?

If so, then glory to God! If not, then it is not too late! If you are unsure, don't worry; we are going to say a prayer that has changed the lives of many! Reclaim your authority, and say this prayer aloud:

Lord Jesus, I come to You just as I am. I am a sinner in need of a Savior. I repent of my wicked ways, and I come to You asking for Your forgiveness. Please accept me as Your daughter. I confess with my mouth that You are Lord, and I *truly* believe in my heart that God raised You from the dead! I commit my life to You. I thank You, Lord, for loving me enough to save my life. Help me every day as I strive to be just like You. In Jesus's name, I pray. Amen!

Hallelujah, you are saved! Please tell someone and get connected under good leadership that is teaching the Word.

Welcome to the family!

Day 2: Lifestyle Change

> I want to know Christ—yes, to know the power of his resurrection and participation in his sufferings, becoming like him in his death, Not that I have already obtained all this, or have already arrived at my goal, but I press on to take hold of that for which Christ Jesus took hold of me. Brothers and sisters, I do not consider myself yet to have taken hold of it. But one thing I do: Forgetting what is behind and straining toward what is ahead, I press on toward the goal to win the prize for which God has called me heavenward in Christ Jesus. (Philippians 3:10, 12–14 NIV)

So, how do you feel? Lost? It's perfectly fine. Most people have a flood of emotions and cannot figure out where to start this wonderful journey. The reality is that you've been on a journey since the day you were born—it has already begun. You just made a decision to reclaim what is rightfully yours.

Application

Take a moment to look over your life—your journey.

Now, begin to bless our wonderful Father for creating a wonderful creation.

Sometimes we can become bound by our pasts and get stuck with the familiar. Release yourself from your past and press forward. You are made new.

Thank God for your life—for your *whole* life, past, present, *and* future!

Day 3: Honeymoon

> Do not be misled: "Bad company corrupts good character." Come back to your senses as you ought, and stop sinning; for there are some who are ignorant of God—I say this to your shame.
> (1 Corinthians 15:33–34 NIV)

In one of our iHeart sessions, I opened the floor to a discussion about the challenges of being a young Christian woman. One of the topics discussed was the challenge of keeping old friends. Understand that when you choose to stand for Christ, everyone will not approve of your decision; as with life as a whole. People will not—I repeat, *will not*—agree and approve of everything you do. So, save yourself energy and time by not looking for it! It's God's approval that matters. What is God asking of you? See below:

> Therefore, "Come out from them and be separate, says the Lord. Touch no unclean thing, and I will receive you." And, "I will be a Father to you, and you will be my sons and daughters, says the Lord Almighty." (2 Corinthians 6:17–18 NIV)

You are now a daughter of the King. In saying that, you now have new expectations. You have to come out from among them and present yourself separate. People do not have to agree with everything you do, but in the end you want them to respect who you are. This only comes by being different and taking a little vacation from the "norm" and getting to know your Father. We can call this the honeymoon stage!

Application

One of two things will happen if you continue to hang around old friends:

1. Hang around them and be corrupted.
2. Separate and be an influence.

Make a choice.

Our number one responsibility as Christians is to be lights to those who are lost in darkness. A light is significant in the darkness ... because it's different.

Day 4: Comparing Your Walk to Other Christians

> So from now on we regard no one from a worldly
> point of view. Though we once regarded Christ in
> this way, we do so no longer. Therefore, if anyone is
> in Christ, the new creation has come: The old has
> gone, the new is here! (2 Corinthians 5:16–17 NIV)

It's easy to fall into the trap of comparing your walk with others. I was speaking with my pastor one day as he was sharing a revelation from God. It was a very simple revelation: do your part. Just think of how much of a difference we could make as a body if we all just did our parts and stopped comparing ourselves and our statuses with others who have *totally* different parts and roles! With that said, there is no reason that you should compare your walk with others. Your relationship with God is between you and God! Yet, if you feel a tug to come out of your comfort zone, then adhere to that conviction! You are a new creature, so you cannot look at things from your old perspective and do things the same way and expect different results.

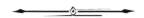

Application

> Change your way of thinking. Today, commit to
> practice dwelling on those things that are true,
> noble, right, pure, lovely, admirable, excellent, and
> praiseworthy (Philippians 4:8).

God is reaching to touch you; *reach* to touch Him. God will exalt you in due time—if you do your part!

Day 5: Temptation (Dating and Sex)

> But he said to me, "My grace is sufficient for you, for my power is made perfect in weakness." Therefore I will boast all the more gladly about my weaknesses, so that Christ's power may rest on me. (2 Corinthians 12:9 NIV)

And here it is. The topic and question everyone's waiting on! How do you deal with the temptation of sex? How can you balance dating without being sexually active? Good question.And I'm still asking myself how I did it! I am not saying that to boast. On the contrary, I'm saying it so that you know that it can be done—and also to let you know that I didn't breeze through it like it wasn't a struggle. I did it through God's grace and His strength.

Application
Give it to God! He will give you strength to wait it out and do it His way. Say this today: "Lord, I give it to You!" Every time that thought comes, say it—even if you say it one hundred times a day! Give Him your weakness.

Don't feel bad about what you're feeling—you're human! God, our great Creator, made us this way! He made us like this for a purpose. Just do not rush your purpose—this purpose—before its timing. Truth be told, you are worth the wait—and God has a guy in place who is willing to wait for his queen. Don't give anyone else what was purposed for that person. He's the one who can handle it.

God cares about you so much that He set a standard not only for you to see your worth but also to *protect* you. He knows that if the wrong person gets the most valuable part of you and does not treasure it with his heart, you will be a wreck physically, emotionally, and spiritually.

Let Him protect you by giving Him your weakness.

Internal Issues

Day 6: I'm a *Big* Deal

In the midst of preparing for one of my iHeart sessions, one night the Lord showed me something. He gave me the equation: a square root sign, and an exclamation point.

Now I'm a lover of math, yet when I saw this I was quite confused. Out of curiosity I asked God, "Lord, what is this?" Shortly after, the Lord began to speak to me and revealed an ongoing challenge among His daughters. Many of us start out with great goals and plans for our lives but become hopeless when we go forth in accomplishing them. A lot of this has to do with the uncertainty of identity. Over the next few days, we will be looking at how to overcome your identity challenges, and we will reveal the solution to the equation at hand.

Application
Today, pray a simple prayer and ask God to remind you of those lost dreams. Then place them before God—give it to Him.

It is my prayer that when we finish this section, you will be motivated like never before because you have resolve in who you are today. I hope you will be challenged to press forward and become who God has destined you to be!

Day 7: What's the Root?

Yesterday I shared with you a mind boggling equation. Reading from left to right, this equation begins with a square root sign. The square root takes a perfect number and shows the root. In other words, it takes something larger and shows the root; it's originality. We all have BIG plans & goals - something that seems larger than ourselves. Yet, as life goes on we become more & more distant from our *original* goals because we hide our true nature, who we are, behind this mask of hurt & pain from our past which results in settling to what we have now - and deep down we are taunted because we know that it's so far off from our *original* plan. In order to inherit the larger things of life (which God has for us), we must allow God to deal with the root. We allow God to deal with the root by identifying the root, which is connected to our whole identity.

Application:
On the following page is a worksheet. It's divided into 3 sections: *Root Issues, (Your Name)'s Destiny/Goals,* and *Transition Steps.*

Identify some things you are not happy with; locate the <u>root issue</u> and write it down.

Next, write down your <u>goals</u>. Where do you want to be in the next few years?

Lastly, write down <u>transition steps</u> that will help you overcome those root issues so that they don't act negatively on your destiny/future goals. What are some things that you can do *today* to move pass this root issue?

Put this worksheet in a visible place (your mirror, door, wall, car dashboard, etc.) to remind you of your goals & how you plan to get there!

God never intended for the pains of your past to cover the plans of your future. You must choose to confront those root issues in order to enjoy a satisfying life designed by God. The pains from your past are nothing but stepping stones, but you, my sister, must choose to step on them not around them.

You're a BIG deal; now deal with ALL of you!!

iHEART Worksheet
I'm a BIG Deal

Root Issue(s):

_____

_____

_____

_____

_____'s Destiny/Goals:

_____

_____

_____

_____

Transition Steps:

_____

_____

_____

_____

Day 8: Uncovered Identity

> The thief comes only in order to steal and kill and destroy. I came that they may have and enjoy life, and have it in abundance (to the full, till it overflows). (John 10:10 AMP)

It is my prayer that yesterday was an eye opener for you & that you took the time to write down those things that have been covered for years, hindering your progression & God's purpose in your life. We have identity challenges because we avoid dealing with what's covered up. It's because we don't want to deal with the pain or whatever it may be. In order to find ourselves in God s perfected will, we must identify the root of the equation. Growth is stunted because we choose to move on rather than facing the issue; which leads to others identifying us. This further leads to you being found in others instead of being found in God. Peer pressure & acceptance from others are tactics of the devil to steal your identity. That's his purpose - to steal and ultimately destroy who you are. If you forget who you are, then you can easily be led and diverted from your *original* path - abundant life. Identity theft happens when the devil uses shame & guilt from our past to stop us from seeing who we can be.

Application:
Do you know what you're capable of? You can change the world with what God has placed on the inside of you! Still don't believe me? Then, ask yourself this: *Why is the devil planning to destroy me?* ... Think about it.

You hold a great treasure on the inside of you. It's time for you to uncover it and live as God purposed: *abundantly!*

Day 9: X Marks the Spot

> However, we possess this precious treasure [the divine Light of the Gospel] in [frail, human] vessels of earth, that the grandeur and exceeding greatness of the power may be shown to be from God and not from ourselves. (2 Corinthians 4:7 AMP)

Have you thought about the question posed yesterday? *Why is the devil planning to destroy me?* I'm reminded of the role of a pirate. A pirate will do whatever it takes to keep treasure hidden from others. Why? Because he wants it for himself. Can you believe that? Even the devil knows how valuable you are & he will do whatever it takes to keep you from seeing that you hold a treasure. A pirate will even go as far as changing the location of the treasure if he senses that someone has uncovered a clue to where the treasure is. Spiritually I'm saying that the devil will uncover or allow you to remember who you are for a second, only to detour you again by presenting a distraction and changing the location of the treasure. We go through these cycles often - back & forth, back & forth - but now *is the time* that you claim your authority and take back who you are! You are a child of God! Don't allow the devil to rule your mind in confusion.

Application:
Right now, choose to take your authority back & realize how valuable you are. A submitted life is a valuable life. Don't allow the devil to tell you that your submission & commitment to God is worthless.

Reevaluate your life and make a list of those things that push you further away from living a submitted life to God & choose to be done with those distractions.

God has a clear-cut plan for your life & it hasn't changed. You hold the treasure! The Bible says that

> In Him you also who have heard the Word of Truth, the glad tidings (Gospel) of your salvation, and have believed in and adhered to and relied on Him, were stamped with the seal of the long-promised Holy Spirit. (Ephesians 1:13 AMP)

We are marked to do great things! Don't allow the enemy to continue to keep what's rightfully yours.

"X Marks the Spot!"

Day 10: At Last

The last part of the equation presented in the earlier chapter is an exclamation point. The purpose of an exclamation point is to show a distinctive indication of major significance; meaning that once you've dealt with the core problems or the root of it all, what's left is marked to be distinctive and of major significance. Once you deal with the issue and find your true identity, your status will be undeniable; and that is what God desires. This is what He expects from you. He wants His children to walk boldly & confidently in the original creation of who they are and not what the world has made them to be. It's hard to deal with and revisit tough & painful issues from our past, but realize that God allowed it to happen for a purpose. It's our make up - it enhances who we are. It's not meant to only cover our scars, but to enhance our appearance as a whole. Don't be afraid to face the naked truth. The Bible states:

> And you will know the Truth, and the Truth will set you free. (John 8:32 AMP)

Now in this instance, Jesus referred to His Word and teachings as the Truth and it is no different here. I am giving you simple principles, according to God's Word, so that you can free yourself from the bondages of your past & live in accordance to God's expectations rather than the world's persuasions.

Application:
After you free yourself, choose to walk with your head held up; confidently. Tell yourself everyday something positive about yourself (i.e. "I'm valuable") and as you go throughout your day,

walk in your God-given authority and speak life to your day. As you do this, walk in expectancy of God.

You're *distinctive*! And wherever you travel & whatever you do will have *major significance*! No more denying who you are! You will have security ... *at last!!*

Day 11: HELP!!!

I'm really enjoying this journey with you & I am even more excited about the new woman you are becoming! I want to encourage you to continue to move forward. Things can be difficult when you choose to take *the* better route for your life by uprooting things. Be encouraged! You are not the only one with daily struggles; we *all* have struggles but the benefit of it all is that we belong to a family that is able to bear the burden when we feel that we cannot. The Bible says:

> We who have strong faith should help the weak with their problems. We should not please only ourselves. We should all please our neighbors. Let us do what is good for them. Let us build them up. (Romans 15:1, 2 NIRV)

You belong to a family of believers that are waiting to help you in those difficult times. Sometimes pride can enter our heart and tell our mind that we are alone ... Then the thought - *"what's the use?"* floods your mind. Many young believers tend to give up at this point in their Christian walk because they fall into that trap of the enemy.

Application:
Don't fall into the state of mind that you are in this alone.
Instead, kill your pride & ask yourself, *"have I reached out to someone?"*

The Bible makes it clear that pride leads to destruction:

> If you are proud, you will be destroyed. If you are
> proud, you will fall. (Proverbs 16:18 NIRV)

Kill your pride and ask someone for help! If you don't know where to start then ask your Pastor. If not there, then send *me* an email. As believers, we are responsible for each other. We are a family. We have the same bloodline - which is the blood of Jesus Christ. Yet, I will never know you need help if you do not tell me *or* if you keep pushing me away when I offer. Pride is a silent killer of many Christians. The enemy uses pride and ego, to send you into isolation, and you fall deeper & deeper because you don't want help. Let that go today! Your progression (the progression you've been praying for) is waiting. God hears your cry for *help;* receive your answer by surrendering your pride & allowing God to use your brother or sister in Christ to *help* you. We're in this together!

Day 12: Surrender *your* will & receive *God's* Strength

> I can do all things through Christ who strengthens
> me. (Philippians 4:13 NKJV)

Many of the core issues of our life revolve around the unwillingness to forgive. It's not that we are not *able* to forgive - the scripture tells us that we can do *all* things through Christ's strength - but it's that we are *unwilling* to offer forgiveness. Operating out of your will and strength can keep you from obtaining the things of God. God gave us our own wills and the freedom of making our own choices. Yet, if we are really looking to living the abundant life, then we must do as the Bible says in Philippians chapter two:

> *Let this mind be in you which was also in Christ Jesus,*
> *(Philippians 2:5 NKJV)*

Although, Christ is the Son of God and has the very nature of God, He had to humble Himself while on earth. The night before His crucifixion He prayed,

> ...Father, if it is Your will, take this cup away from
> Me; nevertheless not My will, but Yours, be done."
> Then an angel appeared to Him from heaven,
> strengthening Him. (Luke 22:42-43 NKJV)

Even though He was the Son of God, He humbled Himself by surrendering *His* will and relying on *God's* strength. As a result,

God sent an angel with the assignment to strengthen Him. God has just what you need, but you will not receive these things operating out of your will and relying on your strength. The obstacles placed in our life are there so that we can rely on God.

Application:
Say this prayer today: *"Lord, not my will, but Your's be done. I surrender to You."*

You may have to say it more than once throughout the day, so purpose to make it a habit to keep that in the forefront of your mind.

The next few days we're going to be dealing with the root of unforgiveness. It is my prayer that you continue to surrender all to Christ & that you will learn how to deal with hurt so that you are no longer bound by *unforgiveness*.

Day 13: The LINK of Bondage - Open the Door

This is titled The LINK of Bondage because when I think about being bound I think of chains. Chains hold us in bondage and one of those links that hold us, spiritually, is unforgiveness. The unwillingness to forgive produces anger & bitterness in your life. Instead of it affecting the one that you're angry with (as you intended), it only affects you & those you love. Think about it ... You may never or very rarely see that person that you are upset with. So, instead of that person receiving all your dirty looks, fits of rage, and bitterness, those around you on a daily basis reap the consequences or his/her actions. Your family, your spouse, your children, your church family, your co-workers, classmates, and/or students - all these people are reaping something that they *never* sowed. Not only that, but the extra energy that you are exerting by lashing out on others is wearing and tearing on your body which makes your Christian walk even harder. But in your mind you're saying, *"No one understands."* Truth is, no one will probably never understand why that person did what they did or why God allowed so much hurt to flow through your heart, but you do have a choice to release that person and/or event and move on with your life. Instead of this being your *tragedy*, allow God to make it your *testimony!!* Choose to be an overcomer!

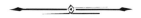

Application:
You cannot undo your past but you can undo your way of thinking. Think back on the situation, and ask God to:

1. Heal the pain that arises at the thought of this person and/or event
2. Show you the purpose of this event

Your garden where you sowed your tears is not barren. You can have a beautiful garden in your backyard but you will never know because of the fear of opening that door. Romans 8:28 tells us that

> ... all things work together for good to those who love God, to those who are the called according to His purpose. (NKJV)

You may not have loved God back then, but He knew one day you would love Him. And because of it, He allowed *ALL* things to work for your good.. Open the door.

Day 14: The LINK of Bondage - Forgive Today

You don't get far in life while holding on to your past. This is a LINK that holds your destiny and goals hostage. Until you let go of that connection of that person or thing, your progression in life will be sluggish. God will place people in your life that will try to help and guide you in moving forward, but you will not excel like you should until *you* make the choice to let go. When you choose not to forgive, you are choosing to carry other people. As women, we are forced to make important life changing decisions, but most of us fail in this area because our mind is cluttered with the issues of our past. We are carrying too much which puts unnecessary weight on your heart - those things you value most. God wants us to live the abundant life; to live the abundant life we must operate in love. To operate in love means we must have a forgiving heart. A forgiving heart is a free heart!

Application:

Meditate on this scripture today:

> In prayer there is a connection between what God does and what you do. You can't get forgiveness from God, for instance, without also forgiving others. If you refuse to do your part, you cut yourself off from God's part. (Matthew 6:14-15 MSG)

At the conclusion of your day, write what this means to you.

What do you want from God? What do you expect of Him? Your live connection to the right LINK rests in the willingness to forgive. Forgive Today!

External Factors

Day 15: Decisions, Decisions, Decisions

Are you sometimes surprised by the actual consequences of your decisions? Do you find yourself going back and forth on a previous decision made? Is your decision *really final* once made? One thing employers tend to seek out in an individual is strong decision-making skills. Decision-Making is a key skill in the workplace, and is particularly important if you want to be an effective leader. It shows the strength of the mind. This is an area that many typically avoid. We fail in this area because we often lean to the easier option rather than the *better* option. We seek convenience instead of cultivation. Fear is the leading factor of why people run away from making the *right* decision.

Application:
When faced with a decision (especially tough ones), ask yourself which route would produce the most *beneficial* growth. That's probably the route that you need to take. Once you perform this filter, then bring it before God in prayer and ask Him to to lead you down the right path & give you peace while traveling.

The Bible says to:

> Seek his will in all you do, and he will show you which path to take. (Proverbs 3:6 NLT)

The King James Version says to acknowledge Him in all your ways … This means that I *must* seek Him in all that I do. The place where He leads you may be uncomfortable and challenging, but I promise you it will be worth it and, as a result you will be a better person. God has the *best* solution for your situation. Remember to seek Him.

Day 16: The Blessing Initiative - Can't We All Just Get Along?

> "You're blessed when you can show people how to cooperate instead of compete or fight. That's when you discover who you really are, and your place in God's family. (Matthew 5:9 MSG)

Nowadays, you find a lot of young women flocking to men - they have a lot of guy friends yet very few girl friends. This may seem simple and insignificant but I find it very important because we are supposed to be there for each other and a woman with a lot of guy friends can end in a dramatic crash of emotions. As women, we like to be acknowledged. We like to feel special. What's wrong with you being the one to make your sister feel special? It doesn't hurt to tell your girl she looks nice. There tends to be a saying that says less women friends means less drama. To a certain extent, I agree because there are some you cannot trust. Yet, lets not single out women. You cannot trust every man as well. With that said, there are some mature individuals that are like a breath of fresh air but you will never know if you continue to stand off and make excuses of why you probably should not connect. Take the initiative to bless you sister.

I suffered from this *syndrome*. When I started dating my husband, I was *even worse* because I thought, "God sent me him. He's my best friend; just what I need." I had a rude awakening when we started to have problems because I didn't like the way he responded to me as I vented to him. He did absolutely nothing wrong. He just responded like a man! LOL I wasn't aware of that until a wise woman sat me down and told me, "Tiffany, you're going to have to branch out and expand your circle because sometimes you need to talk to a girlfriend. Our men mean well, but sometimes they don't fully understand the mind of a woman."

In order for us to expand our circle we must take the initiative of blessing our sisters. Offer a compliment, offer a ride, set up a girls night out, or even plan a trip. Or let's start from the beginning: practice saying hi instead of passing right by that person, as if you didn't see them. The smallest things can make the biggest difference in someone's life.

Application:
Practice blessing others. Don't underestimate the power of reaching out to someone.

When you're having a bad day, don't make the day miserable for everybody. Choose to bless them and you'll find your strength. Your ability to change perspectives and allow God to shine, rests in you blessing others.

Day 17: Lustful Pleasures

> Run from anything that stimulates youthful lusts.
> Instead, pursue righteous living, faithfulness, love,
> and peace. Enjoy the companionship of those who call
> on the Lord with pure hearts. (2 Timothy 2:22 NLT)

We hear the word lust a lot when discussing sex or opposite genders. There's a misconception because lust is not defined by sex. Lust is an intense desire felt - meaning you ask, beg or crave something earnestly. Some people crave knowledge. Other people crave power. These are all lustful pleasures. Lust is conceived in the mind and made alive in the heart which then transitions into fantasies. God wants us to live life in abundance, not in luring imaginations. So, what's the difference of you lusting after something versus pursuing a need of something? Well, lust is a *psychological desire* that fills a temporary need, providing an ending result of pleasure. A need is a *psychological requirement* that provides an ending result of relief.

Application:
They're both undeniable feelings; If fulfilled, which would add to and/or benefit your life?

The Bible commands us to run from anything that stimulates lust and encourages us to run after righteous living, faithfulness, love & peace instead. Lust is easier & more pleasurable at the moment but stressful in the end, while fleeing may be more challenging at the moment but *stress-free* in the end. Instead of focusing on the challenge of overcoming, focus on the relief that you will feel once you overcome!

Please complete the following worksheet:

iHEART Self - Conduct Worksheet
What Do You Choose to Carry On?
Be Honest. Tell the Truth!!

Situation #1: A great night's sleep. You reach for your phone, look at the time and realize that you only have thirty minutes to get to work on time. Amazingly, you are ready and out the door within fifteen minutes. With only fifteen minutes to make it to work and clock in, you are racing through traffic. Then, a car cuts in front of you. Not only does he break your speed, but he's driving 10 miles under the speed limit - in the fast lane. You cannot pass him because there's another car on your right blocking you. How would you conduct yourself in this situation?

_____

_____

_____

_____

Situation #2: Arriving to work 5 minutes late, you clock in. Not long after, you get a call from your supervisor to come into her office. Aggravated and agitated, you go in. She shuts the door behind you and asks you to take a seat. While sitting, you notice papers on her desk and realize that she has plans to write you up. She begins to complain about your tardiness and how you have caused a strain on the company and it's production. You are trying to listen but it is hard to quiet those thoughts of why she is attacking you when Suzy is tardy sometimes three times a week and suffers no consequences for her actions. Why? After your supervisor finishes, she slides the papers across her desk for you to sign. How do you respond?

_____

_____

_____

_____

Situation #3: After a long hectic week, it's *finally* time for a refreshing service at church. You walk in and take a seat. You look to your right and to your surprise the driver that cut you off and *caused* you to be late to work is sitting two rows up. He is an elderly man that can barely get around. He came to church because he feels that this is his only hope to live since his wife recently passed. She passed away the very same day that he cut you off. Then, you look up and you are shocked to see your boss walk through the door. She is looking for answers. The day that she wrote you up she also found out her husband raped her daughter a few years back. Turns out she was having a bad day and you coming in late added to her frustration. Her situation clouded her judgement that day. You both lock eyes. What do you do?

_____

_____

_____

_____

Day 18: Self - Conduct

So, how did you do? Were you ashamed of your actions after reading *Situation #3*? The good thing is that you still had an opportunity to make things right if your actions throughout the week were unpleasing when you arrived to church on Sunday. We must realize that our true ministry is when we leave church on Sundays and go through our week. People are *always* watching you and you never know when you will cross paths again. Not only that, but you will never know when you are entertaining angels. The Bible says:

> Don't forget to welcome strangers. By doing that, some people have welcomed angels without knowing it. (Hebrews 13:2 NIRV)

Practicing good conduct is very important because our lives are *epistles,* or letters, to others. What does your life letter say? Remember, that majority of your life is lived outside the church walls. The pen doesn't stop just because we're not at church Monday through Saturday. As a matter of fact, the Writer may be getting hand cramps throughout the week. Your life counts the most when you are doing your daily activities. How is your conduct? Does your life reflect the culture and traditions of this world or are you living to be the difference? You cannot live two lives. Just because you have a rough start to the day doesn't justify your poor reactions to situations. You have to learn what works for you on those days when you are not feeling up to par. It's your way of thinking that changes to stabilize your outward conduct. Jesus prayed:

> I do not pray that You should take them out of the world, but that You should keep them from the evil

one. They are not of the world, just as I am not of the world. (John 17:15, 16 NKJV)

We are not of this world. We should have that same mindset and it should show in our actions.

Application:
How you approach a situation makes a difference. Approach difficult situations gently. Ask God to give you wisdom as you act. Think & pray before you act.

Pray daily that God sharpens your discernment so that you are able to pick up if a person is just giving you a hard time. If that's the case, then politely excuse yourself.

Don't act out of emotion; seek God's wisdom daily. You have the power to control yourself so that your conduct presents you honorable.

4

Love

Day 19: Love

> Love is patient. Love is kind. It does not want what
> belongs to others. It does not brag. It is not proud.
> (1 Corinthians 13:4 NIRV)

Love. If any of you are like me, then you probably watched fairy
tales when you were a young child and dreamed of a *happily ever
after* life. Then, as you grew into your teenage years you probably
watched and observed other couples *in love* ... real love - love that
endures. Somewhere down the line you probably longed for the
same thing; and there is absolutely nothing wrong with that! Yet,
while yearning and longing for *love,* let me urge you not to forget
about what's really important - you. Many women make lifelong
journeys of trying to do all it takes to attract the right man which
can sometimes lead down the wrong road. Instead of allowing
God to guide your life & lead the right man to you, we sometimes
give off a Jezebel spirit by luring men to come follow us. We wear
clothes that fit in the right places; we cover God's original creation
by using make up as a substitution rather than an enhancement.
The real problem is that we forgot about ourself. We are not content
and satisfied with how God made us. So, to speed the process of
getting a man, we do what it takes; then we are miserable trying to
maintain this man that was never in God's plan for you.

Application:
Practice loving yourself. Tell yourself you're valuable, you're
beautiful. Thank Him for this wonderful creation. ... and genuinely
mean it.

Love is patient. This says a ton. Patience arises from contentment. Are you content within yourself and where God has you? We already live in a fast paced world, so why speed it up? Wait on God and what He has for you. Love does not want what belongs to others. Be content in who you are and where you're at and *he* will find you.

Day 20: Love

It is not rude. It does not look out for its own interests. It does not easily become angry. It does not keep track of other people's wrongs.
(1 Corinthians 13:5 NIRV)

Ever been in a relationship where you just were not happy ... *at all*? I think we've all been there. If you were fortunate enough to get out of the relationship and seek better, did you evaluate why the relationship was *so sour*? Love-making was probably good, but why did you both snap on each other for no reason? Why did it feel like he didn't consider you or understand where you were coming from? Why so much frustration? Does this sound familiar? Do me a favor; re-read the scripture for today ...

Every question that I just asked was in direct alignment to this scripture. The answer to all the questions above is: it's because your relationship did not have love. You both desired each other (infatuation and lust), but it did not rest on *love*. More importantly, *Love (God)*, was not the foundation. With everything going wrong in that relationship, you most likely operated in a way that love does not; by *keeping track* of every argument, misunderstanding, and every *wrong*.

Application:
Before we can love others the way God intended and expects, we must learn how to love ourselves appropriately. Let go of that past relationship. Don't be bound by what happened. Break the chain

and cycle, so that when God sends *him* to you, you'll know how to love *him* the way he needs to be loved.

Let it go. You no longer have to be angry or frustrated. Practice preferring others (in your immediate family, friends, co-workers or classmates) over yourself. Go the extra mile in showing someone God today, by showing *love*.

Day 21: Love

Love is not happy with evil. But it is full of joy when the truth is spoken. (1 Corinthians 13:6 NIRV)

Truth vs. Opinions. When faced with difficult situations, we naturally want to know what someone else would do if they were in our shoes. Yet, we must be very careful to not let their opinion override God's truth. A person can mean well, and what they're advising can make a lot of sense, BUT is it beneficial to you? Does it glorify God? Does it go against what God's truth says? Is it questionable? People's opinions, if not centered around the Word of God, can glorify evil. It feels good at the moment, but can be very dreadful in the long-run. See, God's truth is purposed to make sense in the long-run. It hurts when spoken, but it brings relief *and* it conditions a grateful & thankful heart in following God instead of your emotions. Decisions and life-events centered around emotions are bound to explode in a matter of time. Choose God's way by seeking His Truth.

Application:

Practice telling people the Truth in love. Ask God to give you an extra dose of His grace so that you can extend it to others when sharing His Truth. Remember to release the Truth in right timing. Don't go on your intuition.. Follow the Holy Spirit. He will release you.

As a wife & life long partner to your husband or future husband, he's going to not only expect but also need you to speak truth into his life. Yet, you must make sure that you speak it at the right time and in the right attitude - *love*. The only way to ensure that this is done is to practice. Total submission to the Holy Spirit shown in our actions doesn't happen over night. Successful marriages submit to the Holy Spirit because in submitting to the Holy Spirit, you're submitting to God - *love*.

Day 22: Love

It always protects. It always trusts. It always hopes.
It never gives up. (1 Corinthians 13:7 NIRV)

I am very careful in saying words like *always* or *never*, because when using either one of these words in a sentence you are making a very **BOLD** statement - point blank. There's no in between. Yet, God uses these words. He says love *always* protects, trusts, hopes, and *never* gives up. Wow. This is how God loves & how He desires for us to love. When you enter into a serious relationship, which has great potential to lead to marriage, you <u>both</u> must consider how God loves and be challenged to love your spouse in the same way. The purpose of marriage is not to glorify each other, but it's to glorify our Father above by acting as a reflection of His love. Are you willing to go that far in love?

Application:

Do you really know how much God loves you? When faced in risky situations, are you confident that He will *always* protect you? When you're at your lowest point, do you know that you can *always* trust Him? When put in a completely hopeless situation, do you know that *He is and will always be* your hope? Even when you've given up, do you know that He will *never* give up on you?

There are no ifs, ands, and buts. This is what His Word says. It is definite. God loves you that much, but you must know that and be confident in it so that you can also walk in His love. Love is founded on God. So, it is very imperative to note how He loves so that we, too, can glorify the Father by doing the love walk.

Day 23: Love

> Love never fails … (1 Corinthians 13:8 NIRV)

One of man's greatest fears is failing. It does something to a man when they feel that they have failed the one(s) they love and as a result they back down. Failing implies that one is weak in an area or inadequate. As women, we tend to respond in an emotional way, which can add stress to the situation. In these times we must be reminded of God and who He is *and* we must make a choice to <u>speak</u> who God is, whether it be as encouragement to ourself or life to another soul. We are lights of the world. When darkness presents itself, we must choose to shine. In other words, when someone is drowning in their pity, we must choose to shine and allow God to use us to speak life to them. Failures have led many into depression, which can lead to suicide.

Application:
Don't entertain negativity. Choose to combat it with love. Rely on God's strength and ask Him for His wisdom so that you can be a light to this dying world.

People fail because they try to accomplish things in their own strength and knowledge. As Christians, we have so many things to be thankful for and one is that there are no weaknesses in God because God is love & *love <u>never</u>* fails. Depend on God, and your *happy ending* will come to you. He <u>never</u> fails!!

Maturing

Day 24: Goals

> Good planning and hard work lead to prosperity, but
> hasty shortcuts lead to poverty. (Proverbs 21:5 NLT)

Everyone wants to be successful and everyone *can be* successful. The difference between success and failure is not whether or not you're good at a task. The difference is proper planning. The Bible makes it plain here: when you rush through the planning stage it leads to scarcity. Take being in school - people who become successful doctors and lawyers take the time to not only learn but ace the basics by putting in hard work. They have a clear understanding of where they would like to be, so they sacrifice to prepare themselves for a successful future. People that cheat, fail the final exam because they did not properly plan.

Application:
It is important that you have a tangible/realistic plan in reaching these goals. Where there is no consistency and follow up, your goals become dreams. With that said, complete the worksheet on the following page. This will help you put things in perspective.

Your dreams are not unreachable. All you need is a well thought out plan and hard work to get there. If God placed it on your heart, be encouraged and reach for it. Don't get discouraged by your surroundings and what you don't have. All God is saying is, *"start somewhere, and I will provide the rest."* Your dreams are there for a reason; God is waiting on you to make a move. I'm praying for and with you that everything that God has placed on the inside of you will manifest in this earthly realm for His glory; and that He gives you the strength to stand firm on His Word in the hard times and persevere in the dry times. God's will be done in your life!! Focus is the key in reaching your goals. Don't ever lose sight. Goals do not become Dreams; Dreams become Goals.

iHeart Worksheet
My Goals

Please list your long term goals:

_____

_____

_____

_____

How do you plan to reach these goals, starting today? Please list a due date next to each task.

_____

_____

_____

_____

Notes:

_____

_____

_____

_____

Share your plan with someone who can hold you accountable to ensure that you will reach each goal.

Day 25: Selfish Ambition

For wherever there is jealousy and selfish ambition,
there you will find disorder and evil of every kind.
(James 3:16 NLT)

As women we love to have things our way. We love to be spoiled
and catered to. So, selfish ambition can sneak up on us without us
even realizing what's happening. For example, we will get all dolled
up put on all his (your significant other) favorite things, just so we
can get him wrapped around our finger to do whatever we want.
But when the table turns and he's in need, we either complain or
blow it off because it isn't centered around us. As a result, he takes
a mental note of your reaction during his time of need, so now he
isn't as attentive when you are in need and you take offense ... Now
there is disorder in the relationship all because of selfish ambition.
We are to prefer others over ourselves. This is how we live in the
image and example of Christ. He preferred us over Himself ...

Having a boyfriend just because you like the idea & you don't
want to feel left out when your friends have group dates, is selfish
ambition because you seek a boyfriend to benefit your own selfish
desires rather than genuinely caring about him. This can ultimately
lead to you becoming tangled up in things (such as emotions, living
situations, financial status, etc.) that are hard to come out of.

Application:
Allow God to mold you so that you can stand strong and be
consistent. In other words, God knows what you desire, and He
knows the best way to get there so that you are successful. With

that said, ask God to give you patience during this molding period of your life & completely trust that God will grant your desires, according to His will.

If you truly desire better for yourself and those around you, then you must completely change the way you think. You want to be a successful woman in all areas of your life; and although shortcuts (deceit) may get you to your destination faster, success is developed through the journey to your destination. Success is found in your character. Character is developed through endurance. A successful woman is a consistent woman.

Day 26: Balancing Responsibility - Time Management

> Oh! Teach us to live well! Teach us to live wisely
> and well! (Psalm 90:12 MSG)

To be responsible means not to let those things that you were
entrusted with (whether by God, another person, or yourself) to
slip through the cracks. To be trusted means that people can rely
on you, so it is imperative to know how to support what you're
trusted with even when life seems be uncontrollable. The art of
balancing responsibility rests in your ability to set priorities. When
you choose to ignore what needs attention, that very thing that
requires attention will eventually make itself known; and this
may not happen at the most convenient and comfortable time.
Everything will seem out of control and become overwhelming to
the point where you just don't want to do anything because what
you ignored can no longer be kept silent.

Application:
Complete the following worksheet.

Set your priorities according to importance so that you can
identify what should be considered first. Keep in mind that if you
have responsibilities that cannot be removed from the list (such
as children and/or a family), then you must learn the value of
sacrificing so that your family doesn't feel neglected as well as your
other responsibilities.

Sacrificing does not mean eliminating *all* the other responsibilities
at once. Slow and steady wins the race. You want to always put your

best foot forward in everything you do, so you must learn how to plan accordingly. For Instance:

1. *Family*
2. *Work*
3. *Ministry*
4. *Personal Goals*

I serve my family and I work everyday … but at night when my son is sleep I will work on ministry projects & the next night I will work on my own personal goals … The sacrifice is staying up late but the key is consistency. You don't have to do it this way. This is only an example. Find what works for you and apply it to your life. God did not intend for us to live a life that is overwhelmed. We can live peaceful & joyful lives by implementing practical kingdom habits!

iHEART Balancing Responsibilities Worksheet

List your current responsibilities (children, career, house/apartment, ministry, etc.):

_____

_____

_____

_____

Now list them according to their importance:

_____

_____

_____

_____

Day 27: Balancing Responsibility - Just Keep Swimming

> God is our refuge and strength, A very present help in trouble. (Psalms 46:1 NKJV)

Even when life throws its worse punches, you must know how to keep these things stable. And this may come with many tears. But realize that it is not the responsibilities that are weighing you down; you were gifted to do what you do. It is life that weighs us down. When life becomes heavy, then it seems that everything becomes heavy. Why? Because sinking is a feeling that you cannot ignore. At that point you only want help; because you feel you're in too deep to come out alone.

Application:
Instead of following life's lead in falling apart, take a moment & breathe in.. breathe out. Listen to the voice of the Holy Spirit and feel Christ's embrace. Follow His lead.

You are a follower of Christ, not a follower of life. Sometimes life throws punches not so that we can panic and give up because we do not see help; but it's to show us that *we* have the ability to work through life's difficult situations so that we can get to the Help. As we go through life's tribulations remember that others are watching you to see how you work under pressure. As you follow the example of Christ, what kind of example are you displaying? Is it in representation of Christ? It's not what you do that makes a difference, but it's how you do it. You must show that you can handle what your given by relying on Christ. Although you can't see relief, believe that it's there. When it seems you're sinking in your responsibilities, *do not panic*! Dory from Disney's movie, Finding Nemo, says it best - *Just Keep Swimming*. Help is on the way.

Day 28: Risky Blessings

> Now it came to pass after these things that God
> tested Abraham, and said to him, "Abraham!" And
> he said, "Here I am." Then He said, "Take now
> your son, your only son Isaac, whom you love, and
> go to the land of Moriah, and offer him there as a
> burnt offering on one of the mountains of which I
> shall tell you." (Genesis 22:1, 2 NKJV)

As humans, we do not like to take risks. To take a risk, means that
you are taking a chance of losing something. A Risky Blessing is the
option to bless others by possibly giving your last or something of
value without return. It's a risk because you know that the person
that you're blessing does not have to return the blessing. This is
what makes giving significant and special. This type of giving
makes God smile, because you are doing what people in the Bible
demonstrated. Risky Blessings happen when you make a choice to
give up your will.

Giving up your will allows God to glorify Himself in your life. So,
although the blessing may be a risk at the moment, it's actually a
reward.

Application:
Have you been led to give something of value to someone without
knowing why? Has your will and way of thinking stopped you
from giving? Spend some time in prayer and surrender your will
and thoughts to God. Choose not to ignore the unction to give.
Bring it before God. If the feeling is still there, then maybe you

should consider what you're being led to do. I encourage you to read Genesis 22.

Now, hear me clearly - I am not saying to find something of value to give to a needy person. Not at all. I'm saying that there are times in our life where God will challenge & test us by asking us to give up something near and dear to our hearts. It's your choice to follow the voice of God. It's my advice that says God's voice may not be louder than your thoughts, but sooner or later your thoughts have to bow and subside to God's voice.

Day 29: Risky Blessings

> I once was young, and now I'm old. But I've never seen godly people deserted. I've never seen their children begging for bread. The godly are always giving and lending freely. Their children will be blessed. (Psalm 37:25, 26 NIRV)

People may make broken promises, but God's promises are definite. He never fails! The awesome thing about this scripture is that it applies to everyone - whether you have children, planning to have children or don't desire to have any children. The reward of trusting God at His word is that in the end your children (or those that look up to you) *will* be blessed. There are no ifs, ands, or buts! If you choose to live a life that glorifies God by showing others God's love in blessing them, God's blessing doesn't stop at you. Which further leads me to say, that your life was never meant for you. It was meant for others. God leads us in a way that *always* impacts others.

Application:
Take the risk of making a difference in another's life. It's through your risk that Christ's example and the mystery of the Gospel is seen. Risk-takers are Faith-walkers undercover. Ready to take your faith to the next level?

Our blessing is in our legacy. Jesus left a wonderful legacy and now He is experiencing the *ultimate* reward. He is sitting at the right hand of God - just as God promised Him. Our task on earth is only temporary which gives us an even better reason to leave a greater impact. Why is God so Great? Why does He have all these wonderful attributes? Why does His character give us so much security? Because in this life on earth we will experience *many* trials and testings where we have to have that security in knowing that God is our Rock, Shield, Fortress, Protection, Peace, Joy, Comforter, Sustainer, and the list goes on! We must know this and experience God in every way so that our lives can be a great testimony and an encouragement to others.

Day 30: Expectations Renewed

It is my prayer that these past thirty days have been life-changing for you. I pray that God continues to transform your mind to think like the kingdom agent you were called to be. I pray that how you live your life becomes your first ministry and the most important way of you share the gospel. Purpose to live a life that uplifts God. That's what He desires of you. That's what He expects of you. Let your light shine so that men can see. You are beautiful, you are creative and you are significant. Pursue God at all costs.

Application:
Meditate on this scripture:

> Seek the Kingdom of God above all else, and live righteously, and he will give you everything you need. (Matthew 6:33 NLT)

This scripture *still* carries me through many challenging days; days where I don't feel like praying or reading the Bible because life is _so_ hectic! Then, in the midst of all the traffic going on in my mind, I hear this verse and I choose to press forward. God has exactly what I need and through me seeking Him, I have confidence that He will release what I need at the right time.

Your expectations of life are not crazy. Yes, happiness exists. Yes, you can be successful. Yes, you do not have to struggle. Yes you can do things the right way. It's *all* possible! So, continue to hold your expectations; just make sure that they align with what God desires for you ... His teaching - Righteous Teaching. Hold His teachings close to your heart - *iHeart*

For where your treasure is, there will your heart be also. (Matthew 6:21 KJV)

It is my prayer that your expectations have been renewed.

Notes

Notes

Notes

Notes

Notes

Notes

Notes

Notes

Notes

Notes

Notes

Notes

Notes

Notes

Notes

Notes

Notes

Printed in the United States
By Bookmasters